I0216787

I am little, but my little
legs can do many things.

ယမၢ်ယဲပှၤဆံးဆံးဖိ
ဘၣ်ဆၣ်ယခီၣ်ဖိမၤတၢ်သ့ဝဲအါမံၤ.

My little legs can move.

My little legs can climb.

ယခီၣ်ဖိထီၣ်တၢ်သ့

My little legs can crawl.

ယခီၣ်ဖိစ္စၢ၀ဲဒၣ်သ့ဲ

My little legs can walk.

ယခီၣ်ဖိလဲၤတၢ်သ့

My little legs can jump.

ယခီၣ်ဖိစံၣ်သ့

My little legs can run.

ယခီၣ်ဖိယူၢ်ၤသ့

My little legs can kick.

ယခီၣ်ဖိထူၣုတၢ်သ့

My little legs are strong.

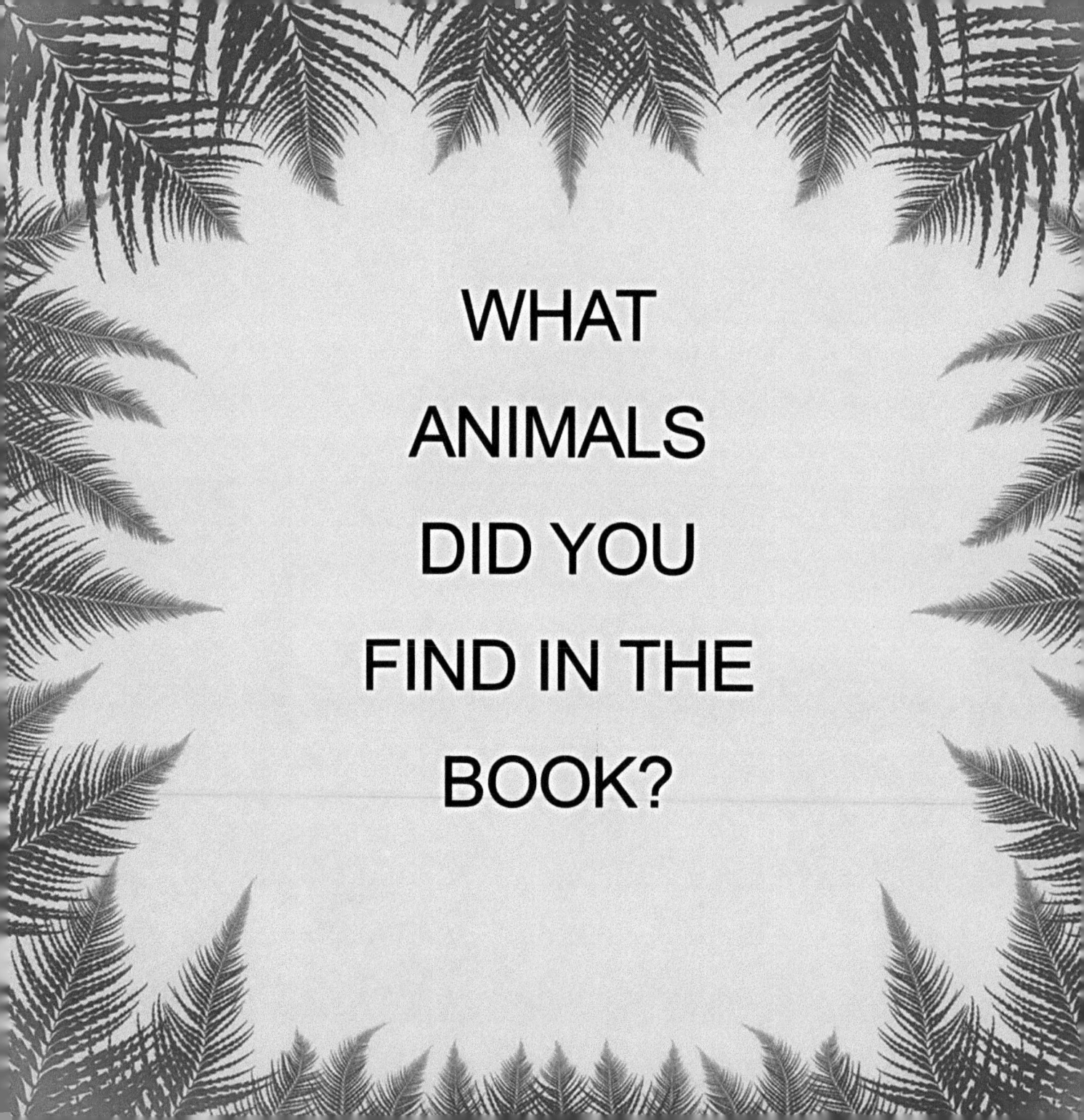

WHAT
ANIMALS
DID YOU
FIND IN THE
BOOK?

www.ingramcontent.com/pod-product-compliance
Lightning Source LLC
Chambersburg PA
CBHW061359160426
42811CB00099B/1141